D1074030

# MR. WINKLE

## The Complete Character Collection

PHOTOGRAPHS BY

Lara Jo Regan

Los Angeles

*To my mother and daughter,*
*two more enchanting characters.*

# CONTENTS

## SOFT SCIENCE
## CUTE COULD SAVE THE WORLD

I first learned of Mr. Winkle in 2002, and became an instant fan. His versatility as a photographic subject seemed impossibly vast. His little pink tongue that lolled out of his mouth in a perpetual gesture of humility made him completely irresistible. At the time, I was a junior high school teacher, and Mr. Winkle became my secret weapon. I loaded up my iPod with an album of Mr. Winkle photos, and when my adolescent students misbehaved or were grouchy, I'd insist they spend a few minutes looking at the pictures. It worked every time; within seconds their mood was better. Mr. Winkle was a veritable panacea.

While people often ask of Mr. Winkle, "What is it?" there is no doubt that whatever he is, he's *cute*.

Whether or not you have a soft heart, it's hard to refute the transformative power in cuteness. Cuteness has both evolutionary and sociological functions that are equally important. While it may be a stretch to say, "Cute could save the world" (though I'd really like to be able to say that), it is undeniable that there is a certain shift enacted when the right kind of cute is inserted in the right place, at the right time. (Mr. Winkle, as far as I can tell, is right all the time.) Anger is diminished, stress abated, smiles increase, people soften.

There are varying scientific and academic associations with cuteness. Kawaii, derived from *The Tale of Genji*, is a culture of cute that permeates nearly all aspects of Japanese society. The popular website cuteoverload.com has a taxonomy of cute spelled out in a growing list of over 30 Rules of Cuteness. Subsets of science and social science – anthrozoology or ethology, for example - are dedicated to studying human-animal relationships, and the increasingly visible field of evolutionary psychology uses science to explain how our thoughts and actions are in the service of evolutionary advantages.

Cuteness is most commonly associated with humans or animals that have noetenic features, like those of an infant: large eyes, big forehead, small limbs, etc. These characteristics serve an evolutionary function to encourage us to have protective, maternal feelings. But cuteness gives back. Cute animals can be therapeutic; they provide comic relief, they teach us how to express love, they spark our imagination, and can even be our physical or spiritual voices. (I refer to my own dog as my physical trainer and anti-depressant.) And while we are more likely to anthropomorphize cute creatures, in so doing we reveal our own thoughts, needs, desires, hopes, and imagination. Mr. Winkle embodies all of these facets of cuteness and more.

It is often said that animals choose us, we don't choose them. Mr. Winkle chose well, indeed, for it was only through the eyes and perception of his human, Lara Jo Regan, that his true greatness was revealed. A renowned documentary photographer with an eye for truth, Regan was observant and sensitive enough to know what gifts Mr. Winkle had and that they needed to be shared. Her extensive background in photography armed her with the creativity and vision that would give Mr. Winkle the platform he needed to work his magic. Regan's photographs of Mr. Winkle call upon a long history of tableaux photography from the Pictorialists of the 19th century to 20th century photographers such as Cindy Sherman. Thus Mr. Winkle came to be contextualized within a dialogue of art and photographic history as well as within the science of cute.

While there have been momentary cute animal fads – such as Knut the baby polar bear or Maru the Japanese cat – Mr. Winkle has been a "cute celebrity" for over 10 years, commanding a massive fan base and countless excited accounts of Mr. Winkle sightings or encounters. He has brought pleasure to millions, and has affected people of all ages. Whether the result of hard or soft science, his je ne sais quoi yields an infectious, insatiable, indescribable desire for more Mr. Winkle. From kitschy to kabalistic, silly to spiritual, Mr. Winkle embodies the canine sublime.

-Micol Hebron, 2011
Chief Curator
Utah Museum of Contemporary Art

# INTRODUCTION

Mr. Winkle entered my life in a manner as mystical and improbable as he is. Lost in an industrial area on the way home from a photography assignment, I spotted an odd tuft of fluff on the side of the road. Moving close enough to take in his diminutive dimensions and enormous, otherworldly eyes, I thought it might be a shipwrecked alien. In the glow of the headlights, this muddy, tattered little creature hobbled straight into my arms, as if he'd been waiting for me all along.

After a year of vet visits and tender loving care, my peculiar pint-sized pal began to meet people on his daily walks, all of whom offered their own theories about his identity. A cable repairman accused him of being a robotic squirrel. An aging hippie declared him a demon from another dimension. An out-of-work actor friend insisted he was not a dog at all, but a cat in a dog suit.

It was these hilarious and inspired reactions from mesmerized strangers that sparked the idea for the "What is Mr. Winkle?" photo series, along with my growing fascination with Mr. Winkle's chameleonic appearance, arresting charisma and profound pathos. His power to heal, enchant and entertain was too overwhelming. He had to be shared with the world.

Without the encouragement of friends and colleagues who perceived me as a serious documentary photographer, I set out to photograph 12 characters for a single calendar, only hoping to immortalize this fascinating creature in some small manner. It was beyond my wildest imaginings that these photos and a companion website would transform Mr. Winkle into an international cult icon, setting off a decade-long demand for "What is Mr. Winkle?" art.

I then became obsessively enthusiastic about character possibilities, but tempered it with a little logic. I felt Mr. Winkle needed to actually look like the character in some way, or be akin in spirit. Lacking those qualifications, the picture had to be downright funny, showcasing Mr. Winkle's inner clown.

Animal identities came first and most naturally, since a multitude of his individual physical features seemed to belong instead to one of his four-legged brethren - like his bushy squirrel tail, full-moon baby seal eyes and proud lion profile. As hundreds of emails to Mr. Winkle poured in claiming the very sight of him helped cure everything from arthritis to bad marriages, I unleashed a parade of therapeutic and mythical personas including the Angel, Buddha and Shaman. Plants, inanimate objects and the more elaborate historical identities soon followed.

Sometimes ideas transpired simply from a random association made with something I saw, felt or thought during the natural unfolding of my life. For example, while looking for an ashtray in a thrift store for a party, I spotted a large fake gold ceramic shell - a spectacularly ugly piece of kitsch I would otherwise dismiss. But it occurred to me that its absurd size made it the perfect fit for Mr. Winkle; if he was placed inside and accessorized with an antennae hairband, he would look like a snail. The "shell" just needed a paint job. So another character was born, which now graces the cover of this book.

Seeing magic and new life in otherwise mundane and pathetic objects was one of the most delightful aspects of the process. The easiest part was Mr. Winkle himself, master method actor, performance artist and supermodel stud he turned out to be. He loved to pose, hamming it up with all his heart. Perhaps it was the fresh chicken strips we kept on every set that inspired him, which he considered acceptable scale pay. But part of me believes the tsunami of affection and attention from his newfound family, friends and fans helped fully heal his past wounds and transform him into a spirit of pure love - which he so eagerly reflects back at us through his pictures. As if he knew his mission, and how to make us see our best selves in his eyes.

Long live the winkle in all of us.

–Lara Jo Regan

This introduction is an updated version of the author preface in *What is Mr. Winkle?*, the first Mr. Winkle book featuring the original 26 characters (Random House, 2001).

FAUNA

An Ancient Koala?

A Race Horse?

A Squirrel?

A Doe in the Snow?

A Lamb?

A Hamster with a Perm?

A Thirsty Camel?

A Ferocious Lion?

A Snowy Seal?

A Newborn Butterfly?

A Bumblebee?

A Hatchling?

A Dust Bunny?

A Cat in a Dog Suit?

A Startled Snail?

A Hungry Orangatang?

A Curious Chimp?

A Sea Lion?

An Oyster . . . or a Pearl?

A Sled Dog?

A Naughty Kitty?

FLORA

A Topiary?

Potpourri?

A Water Lily?

A Dandelion?

A Cauliflower?

A Cactus?

A Cynical Sunflower?

A Bureaucrat?

HUMANKIND

A First Mate?

A Slugger?

A King?

A Punk?

A Ladies' Man?

A Perfect Gentleman?

A Muscle Man?

An Artiste?

A Bell Hop?

A Suspect?

A Cafeteria Lady?

A Clown?

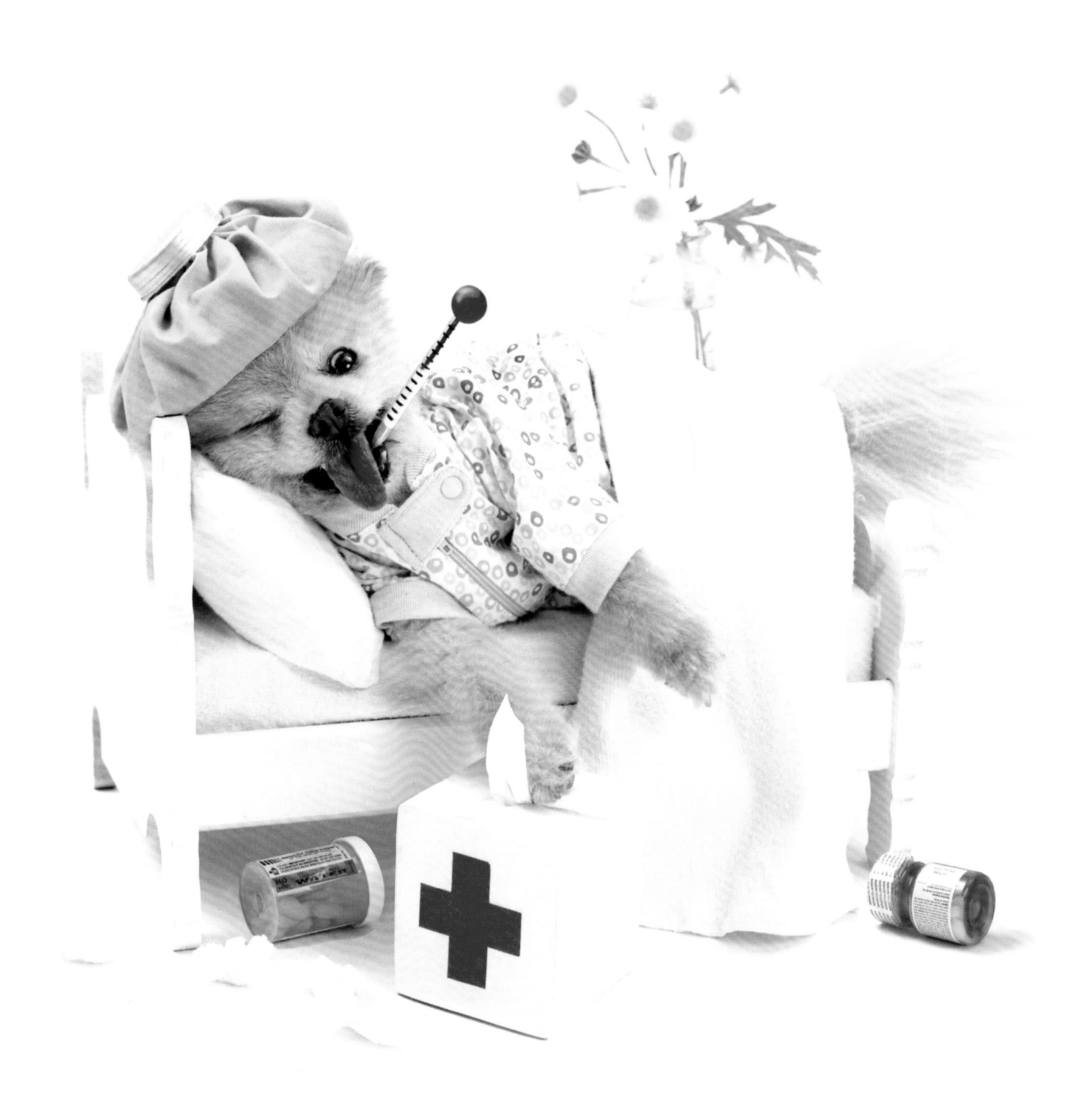

A Patient?

An Infant?

A Best Buddy?

A Girl Scout?

The Fifth Beatle?

A Communist?

A Golden Ager?

A Castaway?

A Chimney Sweep?

A Little Buckaroo?

A Thief?

A Kisser?

A Southern Belle?

A Delivery Man?

An Empress?

A Sophisticate?

A Wandering Waif?

A Prima Ballerina?

A Shaman?

A Boddhisattva?

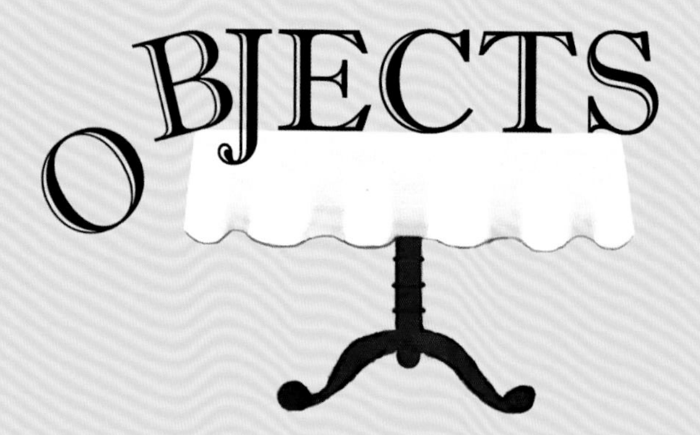
OBJECTS

A Kitch Collectable?

A Jack in the Box?

A Tripod?

A Golf Club Cover?

A Throw Pillow?

A Loofa Sponge?

A Powder Puff?

A Rare Specimen?

A Bedroom Slipper?

A Scarecrow?

A Marionette?

A Hanger?

A Door Stop?

Spray Cleaner?

A VCR?

A Dashboard Ornament?

Head Phones?

A Wind Up Toy?

A Holdiday Ornament?

A Stuffed Animal?

A Pom Pom?

A Pawn?

A Carpet Sample?

# MYTHICAL CREATURES

A Baby Unicorn?

A Victorian Fairy?

A Garden Gnome?

A Sphinx?

A Ghost?

An Alien?

A Troll?

A Wood Sprite?

A Unicorn Shepherd?

A Tiki God?

A Genie?

The Devil?

A Yeti?

A Pumpkin Prince?

A Gargoyle?

Santa Claus?

An Exhausted Elf?

An Archangel?

A Guardian Angel?

HISTORICAL
HEROES

A Patriot?

Otto Lilienthal, German Flight Pioneer

Rosie the Riveter

Greek Warriors at the Battle of Thermopylae

Irish Medieval Monks

Saint Elizabeth, Hungarian Benafactress

Arab Architects of the Islamic Golden Age

Nathanael Greene, American Revolutionary War Hero

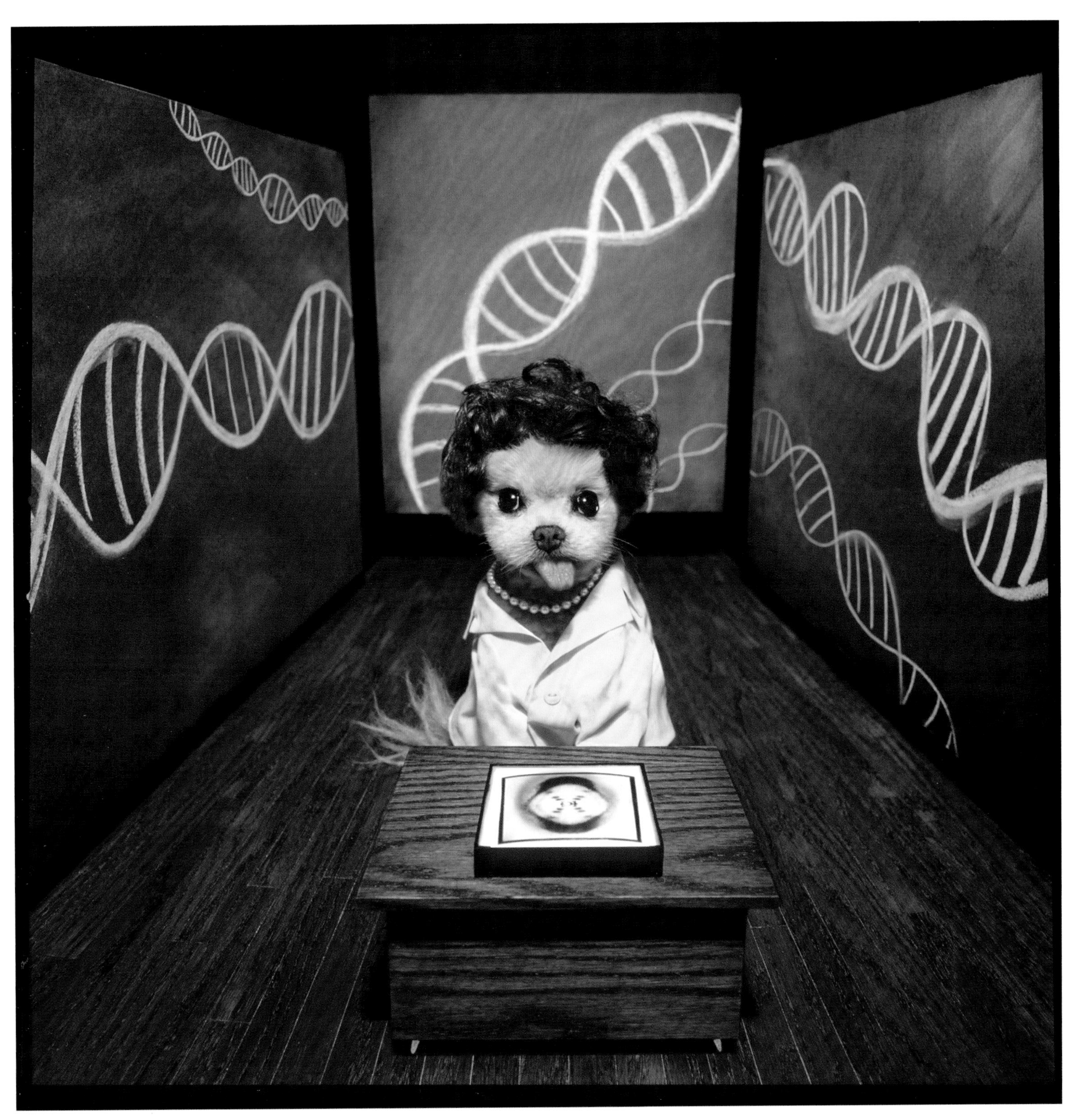

Rosiland Franklin, English Scientist

Alan Lomax, American Folklorist

Miguel Hidalgo, Mexican Revolutionary

Laika, Canine Russian Space Pioneer

Alexander von Humboldt, Prussian Explorer, Scientist

Queen Amanirenas, African Monarch

Philo T. Farnsworth, American Inventor

Camille Claudel, French Sculptor

Murasaki Shikibu, Japanese Writer

Fannie Lou Hammer, American Civil Rights Activist

Matthew Saad Muhammad, American Boxer

# ETCETERA...

A Laboratory Creation?

A Treasure?

A Tourist Attraction?

A Chinook?

A Snowflake?

A Gift?

A Surprise?

A Hallucination?

An Electromagnetic Particle?

The Missing Link?

The Child of a Cloud?

# Mr. Winkle has received thousands of emails offerin

*I think Mr. Winkle is really a dandelion and when the breeze blows soft, gentle and quiet, he spreads his seeds of love, fun and cuteness through the air.*

Due to Mr. Winkle's uncanny resemblance to former Olympic gymnast Cathy Rigby on the cover of the 2001 Mr. Winkle calendar, it appears he is a culmination of the now-lapsed experimental German Olympian bio-genetics engineering program. Recently discovered documents from state archives of the former Soviet Union contain obscure references to funding for a mysterious operation in Eastern Europe named "Das Winkle." Ja? Or Nyet?

He's a pastry.  He's spun with sugar and sprinkled with cinnamon.

**WE BELIEVE MR. WINKLE IS THE NEXT MESSIAH AND I AM WILLING TO SACRIFICE MY SISTER'S PET HAMSTER TO HIM. I ALSO HAVE CATFISH IF HE FANCIES THAT.**

Mr. Winkle is a descendant of the *siogach gabhar*, which is the ancient fairy dog that was originally bred by the famous leprechauns in Ireland. They were the constant companions of these leprechauns and their long tongue was useful in slurping up the puddles of poteen that were left behind when their leprechaun friends had one pint too many, which was most of the time. The only time people saw the *siogah gabhar* was when they found the pot of gold at the end of the rainbow – which absolutely convinces me that Mr. Winkle is related, since discovering him is as magical as finding one of those pots of gold or seeing a rainbow.

Mr. Winkle is a potential cure for cancer. I notice a certain "angiogenetic enhancing" (TM) qualities in Mr. Winkle. I have a molecular biology research team attempting to isolate the "absence of Winkle" (TM) gene, with patent lawyers waiting in the wings. My research tells me it has something to do with a rare enzyme in the tongue.

**Mr.Winkle is a Chihuahua in a polar bear suit that shrunk in the wash.**

heories about his identity. Here are some selections.

Mr. Winkle is a small secret agent disguised as a dog to get clues and pets at the same time.

I suspect he's LUV wrapped in fur.

Mr. Winkle is a manifestation straight from our collective unconscious. His true form will not be known for some time. He is here on earth for all of us.

I think Mr. Winkle is a cloud. Yes, a cloud, catching a falling angel. In catching the angel, he got knocked to ground in some dust. The dust gave him his tan fluffy fur, and his red tongue is the hem of the angel's silk robe he caught on the way down. The angel, in thanking him for saving her, gave him the gift of being so cute he could get the attention of every human so he could help them out.

HE'S A SCIENTIFIC EXPERIMENT GONE CUTE.

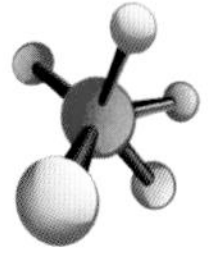

He's a drag queen gremlin

He's a "boggart" – a Scottish spirit that can shape-shift into things.

A lot of debating has gone on as to Mr. Winkle's origin – and I think I finally have it figured out. Mr. Winkle is a Pandora's box . . . once opened the questions will rush forever onward by rampant curiosity. But in the end – in the bottom of the box - there is hope. You are the bringer of hope to people who, in questioning the world, know only if a creature as sweet and special as you exists, then there will always be hope for a better, happier world.

WHAT IS MR. WINKLE? A REMINDER THAT WE DON'T KNOW EVERYTHING.

# ACKNOWLEDGEMENTS

Those who have played an important role in Mr. Winkle's strange and beautiful journey are many, but I would like to devote most of this acknowledgment to Mr. Winkle fans. There are legions of you, as varied and eclectic as the Mr. Winkle character collection itself. This book could not exist without you.

A special thanks to all of you who reached out with letters, emails, and phone calls over the years, which were immensely encouraging. I'm especially grateful to the devoted fans who braved the crowds at book signings, some traveling great distances. I'll never forget the sight of you all lined up, sometimes around the block, often bearing little gifts for Mr. Winkle like modern day wise men paying homage to a newfangled savior. It is hard to imagine my life will ever produce a memory more surreal, amusing and beautiful. Meeting you personally was a privilege and pleasure. I was especially moved by the retired army general who admitted to playing the Winkle's World video every night at bedtime, the sisters who traveled all the way from Japan for a "pawtagraph," the motorcycle gang sporting "Mr. Winkle for President" buttons, the endless waves of wide-eyed children, the many souls suffering from various ailments who shared the ways Mr. Winkle helped ease their pain - including the fellow who claimed his heavy drinking problem was "cured" by Mr. Winkle - and the middle-aged father who summed up the astonishing diversity of surrounding fellow fans by proclaiming Mr. Winkle, "The Great Unifier."

Your ongoing loyal support also made a unique little cottage industry possible, allowing me to ultimately produce my own Mr. Winkle titles without commercially driven compromise – every artist's dream. But I started taking pictures of Mr. Winkle not with business in mind, but because I wanted others to feel what I felt every time I looked at him. There is little that is more thrilling than knowing this intimate communion I try to create on another plane has actually reached into the hearts and minds of others. Thank you so much for letting me know when it did, in so many warm and surprising ways. It made me feel connected to something bigger than myself, while giving me a wonderful sense of completion.

*–Lara Jo Regan*


I would also like to extend my gratitude to those listed below who helped bring the images in this book to life, or who contributed in other special ways to the story of Mr. Winkle.

Mr. Winkle
David DiMichele
Michael Peter Regan
Daryl Redalieu
Mika Mingasson
Chris Hopkins
Fionn Zarubica
Olivia Ramirez
Dara Folkert
Cyrus Chatres
Constance Schlobohm
Wayne White
Betsey Kearns Anderson

Bernd Heinl
John Dutton
Liza Persky
Rosie O'Donnell
Beth Lapides
Greg Miller
Michael Patrick King
Jane Pauley
Walter Stone
Annie Stepak
Mauri Blackwell
Murray and Fred
Jan Nichols

Debra Turner
Wheely Willy
Vital Vayness
Kate Klimo
Courtney Silk
Guy DiMichele
Jeanne Morse
Dr. Robert Lesser
The Wirkkalas
Micol Hebron
Keith Stone
Lori Golden
Dennis Arp

Jillian Reynolds
Michael Kotchman
The Today Show
PETA
Sarah Casey Newman
Bettijane Levine
Marco della Cava
Karen Sandstrom
Cynthia Hubert
Donnell Alexander
Misha Davenport
Niva Chonin
Nigel Cox/Nathan Marsak

The fascinating stories behind the heroes
Mr. Winkle portrays in Chapter 6 can be found in

**A Winkle in Time**
**Mr. Winkle Celebrates the Underdogs of History.**

To learn more about this book and other Mr. Winkle titles visit

## www.mrwinkle.com

## Mr. Winkle welcomes Facebook friends!



Graphic Production: Pay Fan

Published in the United States by All Things Winkle LLC.

Los Angeles, California
626 398 1275

www.mrwinkle.com

ISBN-13: 978-097992969-4

First Edition 10 9 8 7 6 5 4 3 2

Printed in China

# BIOGRAPHIES

**Lara Jo Regan's** career as a photographer has been uncommon and diverse, achieving serious acclaim and respect across several disciplines. With a background in anthropology, journalism, fine art and film, Regan's work combines painterly aesthetics with closely observed behavioral studies and social commentary, a signature style she has applied to everything from impoverished Appalachians to the Hollywood elite. Her interpretive coverage of American culture has been regularly commissioned and published by many of the world's leading magazines such as Time, Newsweek, Life, and is widely collected an exhibited. She is the recipient of many of her field's highest honors, including the coveted World Press Photo of the Year.

Ironically, Regan later became known for creating a cultural phenomenon rather than covering one, as the artist behind the Mr. Winkle photo collection. Featured in books, calendars and collected artwork, the unique images transformed her canine muse into an internationally renowned and respected cult icon representing the beauty and potential of stray animals.

Regan is also the creator of mrwinkle.com, an enormously popular and groundbreaking website launched in 2000. A year later, Mr. Winkle was named "Internet Celebrity of the Year" by Time magazine's online publication, at which time mrwinkle.com had garnered over 40 million hits, totaling over 70 to date. Mr. Winkle is credited by many as the first celebrity animal in history (and one of the first celebrities, in general) whose fame was spread by a website and viral internet culture. Mr. Winkle and Regan were also the first author-animal team whose book tours attracted record-breaking crowds at signings, inspiring the creator of the popular show Sex and the City to incorporate the strange and amusing phenomenon into an episode.

She is a long-time resident of Los Angeles where she lives with her family.

**Micol Hebron** is an artist, curator, educator and writer based in Los Angeles. Originally from Northern California, she studied art history, visual arts and theatre at UCSD, UCLA and the Academia Di Belle Arti in Venice, Italy, receiving her MFA from UCLA in New Genres in 2000. Professor Hebron has exhibited, performed and lectured throughout the U.S. and Europe, and writes for numerous international art magazines. She is an Assistant Professor of Art at Chapman University and adjunct Chief Curator at the Utah Museum of Contemporary Art, where she is the proud curator of a retrospective exhibition in 2012 of Lara Jo Regan's Mr. Winkle photographs.